NOBODY WANTS
TO EAT THEM ALIVE

NOBODY WANTS TO EAT THEM ALIVE

Ethical Dilemmas and Media Narratives on Domestic Rabbits as Pets and Commodity

GAYANE F. TOROSYAN AND BRIAN M. LOWE

NOBODY WANTS TO EAT THEM ALIVE
ETHICAL DILEMMAS AND MEDIA NARRATIVES ON
DOMESTIC RABBITS AS PETS AND COMMODITY

iUniverse books may be ordered through booksellers or by contacting:

iUniverse
1663 Liberty Drive
Bloomington, IN 47403
www.iuniverse.com
1-800-Authors (1-800-288-4677)

Because of the dynamic nature of the Internet, any web addresses or
links contained in this book may have changed since publication and may
no longer be valid. The views expressed in this work are solely those
of the author and do not necessarily reflect the views of the publisher,
and the publisher hereby disclaims any responsibility for them.

Any people depicted in stock imagery provided by Thinkstock are models,
and such images are being used for illustrative purposes only.
Certain stock imagery © Thinkstock.

ISBN: 978-1-5320-1827-5 (sc)
ISBN: 978-1-5320-1828-2 (e)

Library of Congress Control Number: 2017903204

Print information available on the last page.

iUniverse rev. date: 03/10/2017

For Dr. Ricardo De Matos of the Cornell University College of Veterinary Medicine for saving the life of Napastak "Bunny" Torosyan

PROLOGUE

In the unseasonal warm December of 2015, residents of the small college town of Oneonta in the Southern Tier of New York noticed a group of white-and-grey domestic rabbits lounging under shrubbery on front yards, running across busy Maple Street, or begging for broccoli from kind neighbors. One of my friends posted a photo of the rabbits on social media, so my husband Hovhannes and I started checking on them to see what can be done to help these apparently abandoned pets. During one of these evening walks we saw a rabbit that looked slightly different from the other black-and-white or white-and-grey members of the group. With an egg-shaped head, a smooth white body and a line of silver sprinkles dotting her back, she emerged from a moonlit alley to partake in the feast of the strays, then quickly turned around and disappeared back into the dark. We named that rabbit Cutie.

Compassionate neighbors encouraged me to contact The Rabbit Resource, the New York chapter of the House Rabbit Society, for advice on trapping and rescuing the bunnies before the weather turned cold. Chapter leader Davida Kobler and her fellow volunteers took time from their busy schedules to coach us in rescue techniques. It took a brand-new humane trap and some banana bait to bring the first five rabbits out of the elements just before the winter holidays. An appointment was booked right before Christmas with Dr. Barbara Roach of The Village Veterinarian Hospital in Canastota, New York, to get three of the rabbits checked and scheduled for spay or neuter surgeries. Dr. Joanne Puritz of the Oneonta Veterinary Hospital fostered the first two rescued females at her clinic, and placed them in good homes before the holidays.

The moment we returned from our two-hour trip from Canastota with surprisingly clean bills of health and no pregnancies, the neighbors called to report that the sixth rabbit was rescued and named Holly. She was immediately scheduled to have surgery with the others.

On January 7, 2016 Hovhannes left for his daily commute to work in Norwich with a car full of rabbits in affordable black and blue carriers, planning to drop them off at the clinic near Oneida and to bring them back the next day after work. A few hours later I received a call from Davida Kobler telling me that Cutie was "very pregnant" and very stressed, so I had to rush to the clinic and bring her back home. While driving towards Oneida, I received even more troubling news: Holly's blood work did not look good at all. Subsequent surgery revealed that she was carrying a litter of three deceased fetuses in a raptured uterus, which seriously compromised her internal organs. Dr. Roach consulted with Cornell University's Head of Exotic Pet Service Dr. James Morrissey and spent several hours in surgery, fighting for Holly's life. The bunny made full recovery, but her tail dried out and fell off a few months later in foster care provider Sarah Muccigrosso's home in Corning. Holly must have suffered a predator attack while trying to survive pregnant and scared in the streets of Oneonta.

January 11, 2016 was a memorable day: Cutie gave birth to four pink wiggly babies in a cardboard box lined with her fuzz. The following nine months were busy feeding, cleaning and taking care of a double-dose of rescued rabbits in the spare bedroom of our small house. By mid-September, all eight of the Oneonta rescues were adopted by families living all over the state of New York.

My co-author Brian Lowe and I both have rabbits at home, but in our free time we teach at the State University of New York College at Oneonta. Dr. Lowe teaches in the department of Sociology and has published a significant body of scholarship on animals and society. My area of expertise is media, but I have come to embrace animal advocacy through personal experiences and volunteer work.

As Cuties babies turn one year old tomorrow, I want to thank the truly multicultural community of their foster and adoptive families united by a firm belief that rabbits deserve the same humane and ethical treatment as other companion animals. The present study is not about them, but the publication of this book is inspired by a deep gratitude to the veterinarians, rescuers and caregivers who help rabbits live longer, better lives. Their selfless efforts and unconditional love for animals make me believe that the world is changing towards adopting higher standards of humanity and respect for all forms of life. The present study adds a glimpse of hope for that kind of future.

Gayane Torosyan
Oneonta, NY

CHAPTER ONE: INTRODUCTION

At one of the farmers' markets in upstate New York, a meat and poultry vendor proudly displayed photographs of animals raised and slaughtered in conditions that appear far more humane than those at factory farms. On an older photograph, the farmer's daughter was featured at a young age, holding a small rabbit in her hands. The father assured that his children were used to the idea of treating young animals as pets and later eating their meat.

One of the recent additions to the photo display, along with young piglets and lambs, was a haunting image of a white mother rabbit standing on her hind legs, looking at her newborn kits curled up in a fuzzy nest. Next to the photograph was another one, featuring the vendor himself, proudly holding a few freshly killed rabbits by their hind legs. His now grown daughter, sporting a tee shirt that read "Eat Grass Fed Meat," commented on the photo: "Nobody wants to eat them alive!"

As the popularity of rabbits as domestic pets increases worldwide, a parallel perception of those prey animals as commodity remains equally dominant in public discourse. Particularly, this dual perception can be documented through an analysis of news media, which scholars consider as a form of recorded history (Berger, 2011) and one of the foundations and reflections of socially constructed reality (Tuckman, 1978; Fishman, 1980; Gamson, Croteau, et.al, 1992).

This study uses quantitative content analysis of worldwide news media coverage as a basis for a measure to determine which narrative appears to be dominant within public discourse. A coding system is used to classify newspaper articles according to their themes, followed by a numeric analysis of the chronologically ordered data for changes and trends over the period of 21 years.

CHAPTER TWO: THEORETICAL OVERVIEW

Sociologists have been questioning the effectiveness of studying nonhuman animals in general, and the legitimacy of doing so for advocacy purposes in particular Peggs (2013). The conclusion has been that sociology has a lot to offer to the area of human-animal relations, and scholars in this field have a key role to play in enabling this work to move from margins to the core of published sociological inquiry (Peggs, 2013, p. 591).

York and Longo (2016) believe that sociologists tend to incorporate animal studies into the domain of their discipline in an effort to expand understanding of the world and generating new questions. Kathy Rudy (2011) takes it further by describing the contemporary animal rights movement as a multi-faceted effort ranging from vegetarianism to animal liberation, arguing that in order to achieve their goals of ending animal testing and factory farming, animal rights activists need to recognize the emotional attachment between humans and their companion animals. Similar to the present study, Rudy explores five realms of animal-human interaction: as companions, as food, in entertainment, in scientific research, and clothing, suggesting that the nearly universal stories we tell about animals will lead to broadening the acceptance of animal advocacy, and inspire new ethical standards to improve the lives of animals on the planet.

Arluke and Sanders (1996) argue that (Western) humans categorize and rank nonhuman animals through a sociozoologic scale "...according to how well they seem to "fit" in and play the roles they are expected to play in society. How well animals seem to know their place and stay in it will determine worth and position on the social ladder (Arluke and Sanders, 1996: 169)." In short, these rankings are not based on phylogenetic grounds (biological distinctions), sentience or other bases for self-awareness or suffering, but on how well animals contribute to reinforcing the social order. This binary division is based on placement and perceptions of dangers posed, either as good ("... good animals have high moral status because they willingly accept their subordinate place in society, with some able to enjoy their niche while others dutifully comply with it") and bad ("...have a low moral status because their subordinate place is unclear or because they no longer remain quietly out of sight and distant from people") (Arluke and Sanders, 1996: 169-170). These binary divisions are further divided into more nuanced categories (pets, instrumental animals, freaks, vermin and demons) rooted in a dualistic moral reasoning:

> "That societies perceive animals as good or bad indicates that social constructions typically dualistic...We construct images of good and evil, respectable and disreputable, friend and foe, desirable and undesirable, and countless other morally laden oppositions. Each social construct necessarily implies the existence of its opposite and depends on this opposite for its meaning. Significantly, these oppositions are taken for granted in everyday moral communication and, consequently, exert much force in our lives. They do so by prompting us to take certain actions, even if inconsistent, and then to justify these actions towards animals. Just as the sociozoologic scale justifies inconsistent treatment of animals, the construction of good and bad animals can similarly justify inconsistent treatment of humans. Dualistic thinking, then, about animals and their place in

society is useful as an instrument of social control"
(Arluke and Sanders, 1996: 170).

Arluke and Sanders contend that human societies will categorize animals along this "good and bad" continuum, limiting possible locations in the social imaginary (Taylor, 2003) of animals. "Good" animals are either highly anthropomorphized as pets or conversely are treated as instrumental "tools" in that they are utilized for human benefit (as in agriculture and and/or laboratory experiments). "Bad" animals include those that are physically bizarre ("freaks"), are perceived as dirty because they threaten some aspect of the social order ("vermin"), or become "demons" because they pose dangers to humans.

These classifications are often related to other tensions within the social order: the late nineteenth century decimation of non-native sparrows in the United States "mirrored debates over immigration" and occurred without evidence that sparrows were a threat to either humans or their economic enterprises (Arluke and Sanders, 1996: 180). Similarly, Arluke and Sanders contend that much of the contemporary anxiety expressed in the United States and Canada over Pit Bull Terriers is because these dogs have become associated with urban minorities and illegal activities (particularly controlled substances), obscuring the reality that these same breeds were celebrated as companion animals for both families and troops at the beginning of the twentieth century (Arluke and Sanders, 1996: 183-185; (Arluke and Bogdan, 2010). Arluke and Sanders conclude that the sociozoologic scale "is a type of story that humans – with the help of animals – tell themselves and each other about the meaning of "place" in modern societies" and that "the social construction of animals are highly flexible and rich symbols", thereby challenging any assertions that the classification of specific breeds or types of animals as being permanent and/or immune to change (Arluke and Sanders, 1996: 186).

The potential for a sociozoologic scale to be simultaneously socially enduring and "highly flexible" raises significant questions about how certain animals are moved either between categories of "good" or "bad" and/or within them. For example, Arluke and Sanders consider animals utilized as tools because their functions are highly valued, but are made instrumental through any denial of individuality: "To become tools...their animal nature must be reconstructed as scientific data or food. To accomplish this transformation, animals must be deanthropomorphized, becoming lesser beings or objects that think few thoughts, feel only the most primitive emotions, and experience little pain (Arluke and Sanders, 1996: 173)." This process is literally institutionalized as *superobjects*, laboratory animals that are "virtual clones of each other, manufactured and customized to meet sciences needs, and submissive and cooperative to make their use in experiments easy (Arluke and Sanders, 1996: 173)."

However, such a process may be reversed if such an artificial animal escapes from its laboratory setting, instantaneously becoming "vermin" to be contained or killed. In short, the location of an individual animal, breed, or specific species is not fixed, but is subject to events (such as an escape) or perceptions (as in the cases of the aforementioned Pit Bulls and sparrows). However, the sociozoologic as articulated by Arluke and Sanders does not explicitly account for one species simultaneously occupying both "good" and "bad" locations, as in the case of rabbits. Rabbits have traditionally been hunted by elites and non-elites, raised as agricultural animals for their meat, and used in laboratory experiments. Rabbits have also been kept as pets, and more recently have been the subject of a drive to keep rabbits in homes and not regulated to outside hutches. Michael Moore captured this multi-positional status in his film *Roger & Me* (1989), when he filmed a woman in Flint, Michigan selling rabbits as "pets or meat", killing and skinning a rabbit before Moore and his camera (an incident that Moore states is among the most commented upon when *Roger & Me* is publically screened).

Beyond the question of animals, there is the question of what actions or practices animals are subjected to. Arluke and Bogdan (2010) contend that their survey of photo postcards taken in the first third of the twentieth century in the United States revealed that Americans were not squeamish or unsettled by the photographic evidence of the slaughter of animals for consumption. Moreover, such images were probably reflective of a wider reality for many Americans, either living on farms or raising some animals (particularly chickens) in more populated settings for their own use that many Americans had participated in the killing, dismemberment, and preparation of animals for consumption. In short, the early twentieth century American was apparently unfazed and accustomed to the sight of animals being killed and consumed, and therefore did not find the circulation of such images embarrassing, unsettling or undesirable. However, the same period also revealed that larger slaughterhouses, first created in the late nineteenth and early twentieth century's, became conscious of their own representation:

"...we did not encounter any candid interior images of large processing plants taken by local photographers. Plant owners were under attack by reformers and were not open to having outsiders with cameras shoot their operations. Meatpackers such as Swift and Armour mounted publicity campaigns to counter negative portrayals...Some of their propaganda was in the form of photo postcards, but bulk production for wide distribution required that images be printed rather than photographed. However, Swift did a series of sanitized, touched-up, and otherwise manipulated photo postcards to show the cleanliness of the operation as well as the good working conditions. Ironically, one in the series showed the stables where the draft horses that pulled delivery wagons were kept in luxurious quarters. The conditions shown for the horses greatly exceeded the well-being of the workers, not to mention the cattle and hogs being proceeded nearby. The series of postcards was an attempt to rebut the attacks made on meatpackers by muckrakers for the poor sanitary conditions animals faced and the horrific assembly-line environment workers endured" (Arluke and Bogdan, 2010: 102-103).

The significance of the aforementioned findings is that the large-scale meatpacking industry became aware of the significance of the importance of "perception management" early in the twentieth century and therefore attempted to manage the quality and circulation of images related to the slaughter and processing of animals form that historical point forward. Therefore, it may be reasonable to imagine that images of animal suffering, especially animals that may be objects of sympathy, would be controlled by large-scale actors (and others).

Arluke and Bogdan argue that rabbits were one of these species surrounded by ambiguity in that they were simultaneously slaughtered for food, used for fur garments, and kept as pets (often involving the same species):

> "Rabbits were both popular house pets and raised to be killed to supply fur for the garments industry and meat for consumption. Rabbit fur became fashionable in hat design as well as trim on coats. Rabbit meat was more popular in the first third of the twentieth century than it is today. During World War I and the Great Depression, as well as during World War II, the government encouraged people to raise rabbits for their own table and to supply soldiers.
>
> The Flemish giant rabbit (males can grow to twenty-two pounds)...was imported to the States in the early 1890s and began appearing in livestock shows around 1910. The National Federation of Flemish Giant Rabbit Breeders, formed in 1916, promoted the breed. It is referred to as a "universal breed" suitable for breeding, fur production, and pet keeping...However, raising rabbits for meat declined after World War II, saving it from the industrialization experienced by other meats" (Arluke and Bodan, 2010: 105-106).

We suggest that the transitions between rabbits perceived

primarily as a resource (as meat and/or fur) and pest (a destructive or threatening animal) and subsequently as a companion (as pet or as fictional protagonist) is explained partially through the fluidity of the symbolic, cultural, and social boundaries to which rabbits have been related. In general the constructivist tradition (Berger and Luckmann, 1966 ; Best, 2007) suggests that the societal understanding of an object, practice, and/or phenomena is subject to change over time if the socially constructed categories are not maintained or are altered by social actors, and should not be understood as being permanent. Moreover, such symbolic and cultural categories may be subject to a binary logic (see Douglas, 1966; Alexander, 2010) in which objects, practices and/or phenomena are subsumed within broad categories of purity and goodness or danger and pollution. In the case of symbolic and cultural understandings and perceptions surrounding nonhuman animals the relative positions of specific animals may move over time, although such boundaries are not equally fluid: for example, it is unlikely that the consumption of dog meat will become acceptable in the United States in the near future because of the strong negative emotional responses invite (see Herzog, 2010). Conversely, the relative position of other animals, such as horses has moved from a common part of everyday life to an animal associated with bucolic rural areas. We argue that the relative position of the rabbit as object (as resource and/or pest) to subject (real or virtual companion) can be partially accounted for through the movement of symbolic boundaries.

CHAPTER THREE: METHODOLOGY

The method of this study is content analysis conducted on the results of a keyword search through the LexisNexis Academic online database. Each one of the resulting1000 stories was examined from a narrative perspective, using Semiotic analysis as a qualitative tool for classification and labeling.

Semiotic analysis is a research methodology that studies the role of signs as part of social life. The laws of semiology are borrowed from Saussue's (1983; 1974) linguistics that has earned a stable place in the field of human knowledge thanks to structuralism.

The Russian folklorist Vladimir Propp (1927/1968) suggested that all human narratives can be compared to fairy tales and analyzed through their sequential structure or the chains of events forming the plot. The word "syntagm" is derived from the Greek "suntagma" or the French "syntagme" and means "chain." Based on Propp's findings, syntagmatic analysis provides a method for categorizing plot structures according to basic actions or "functions," as well as a method of breaking down characters into seven basic types. Propp maintains that there are only 31 standard "functions" in any fairy tale and, consequently, any other type of cultural narrative, including news.

The content analysis is based on the theoretical premise of history as a record of current events (Berger, 2011), and a more critical perception of news media as a form of socially constructed reflection of reality. A diachronic convenience sample is drawn from an exhaustive database of news stories chronologically dated from 1990 to 2011 and containing a reference to "rabbits" in any form or context. The database is generated through a LexisNexis Academic search with the key word "rabbit" and an international scope of media outlets. Each story is analyzed semiotically to determine in which one of the following categories it belongs:

A) Ethical: rabbits as pets, subjects of rescue, or otherwise humanely treated animals; excluding meat production
B) Commodity: rabbits as a source of food, fur, or other materials
C) Medical: rabbits as subjects of laboratory tests, including pest control viruses
D) Environment: wild rabbits as pests or nuisance, including hunting
E) Entertainment: rabbit characters in literature, film, and other forms of cultural discourse
F) Change: shifting attitudes towards rabbits from object to subject (indicated as a positive value in the story count) and vice versa (indicated as a negative value)

The categories listed above are mutually exclusive, but can be loosely organized into two subgroups: 1) rabbits as subjects and 2) rabbits as objects. The first subgroup includes the Ethical, Entertainment and positive values of Change categories, while the second group includes Commodity, Environment and the negative values of Change categories. Inter-coder reliability was achieved through an agreement to consider the content of each news story in its "inverted pyramid" scheme by first examining the lede paragraph to determine the focus, and continuing with the remainder of the text for further detail and clarification. Answering the basic journalistic questions of Who, What, When, Where, Why, How allowed to identify the characters and plot of each story. Duplicate stories appearing in the database were dismissed from the count, thus bringing the total number of examined stories to 942. That number includes 234 stories in the Ethical category, 163 stories in the Commodity category, 74 stories in the Medical category, 258 stories in the Environmental category, 119 stories in the Entertainment category, and a total of 10 stories that were coded as Change.

The semiotic analysis of each news story is conducted with syntagmatic and paradigmatic tools (Berger, 2011) that include functions such as Villany, Lack, Struggle, Victory, Rescue, etc.; dramatic personae, according to Vladimir Propp's (1927/1968) scheme, such as Hero, Villain, Donor, False Hero, Helper, etc.; as well as stated and implied paradigmatic opposites such as danger-safety, fragile-strong, cannot be reconstructed (healed)-reconstruction (healing) possible, etc. Because of the vast number of items on the database, the results of this analysis are abbreviated into simple codes to match the six categories listed above.

CHAPTER FOUR: NARRATIVE CATEGORIES

Before proceeding to the numeric analysis of the data, it seems necessary to provide a brief qualitative overview of the major characteristics and examples representing each narrative category. The LexisNexis Academic search on "rabbits" yielded close to 1000 English language print news stories dated from 1990 to 2011 from major world publications. Organized from oldest to newest, the set of stories was exhaustively analyzed for content. Each story was briefly described for the nature of its narrative and assigned a resulting code to match the six categories outlined earlier: A) Ethical, B) Commodity, C) Medical, D) Environmental, E) Entertainment, and F) Change.

Using the method of content analysis, the overall news coverage was thus categorized and numerically examined to determine which narrative appears to be dominant within the sampled segment of the media's reflection of public discourse, and what trends, if any, are exhibited throughout time. The results of the numeric count of stories in each category are shown on the table in Fig.1.

Number of Observations Per Category

Year	ETHICAL	COMMODITY	MEDICAL	ENVIRONMENT	ENTERTAINMENT	CHANGE+-
1990	7	1	5	16	5	0
1991	0	13	1	9	11	0
1992	8	2	1	5	2	0
1993	4	1	1	6	3	0
1994	5	2	0	5	4	0
1995	6	14	21	27	1	0
1996	3	2	8	32	5	0
1997	17	5	5	16	5	0
1998	10	13	2	11	2	0
1999	15	13	0	9	11	2
2000	20	8	0	4	6	2
2001	15	2	1	9	2	0
2002	9	6	3	22	3	0
2003	3	6	6	12	4	0
2004	3	10	4	4	7	0
2005	13	6	1	11	3	1
2006	21	16	3	8	2	4
2007	18	11	9	15	7	0
2008	13	10	1	12	8	0
2009	4	11	2	18	14	-1
2010	28	7	0	5	13	0
2011	12	4	0	2	1	0
	234	163	74	258	119	NET 8
						TOTAL 10

Fig. 1

A) RABBITS AS PETS, OR THE ETHICAL CATEGORY

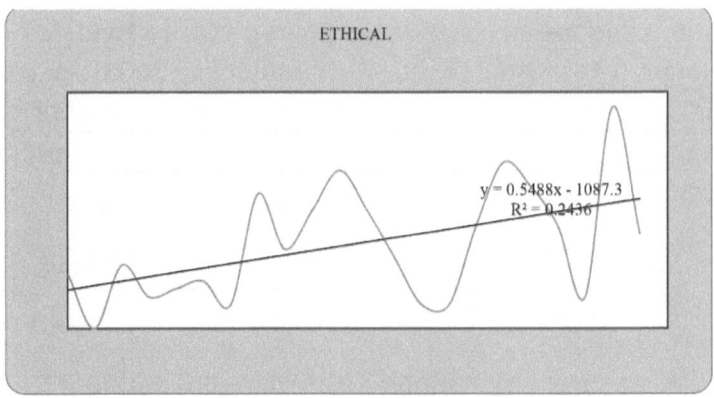

Fig. 2. The vertical axis indicates the number of stories per year

The majority of articles in this category describe pet rabbit ownership as a rewarding yet demanding experience, emphasizing the dangers of adopting or gifting animals around the Easter holiday, which often leads to tragic consequences with animals abandoned or dead after their novelty runs out in a month or two (Neil, 2007). The plot characters associated with rabbits in this category can range from Victim to Prize or even Hero, with functions including Lack, Struggle, Victory, and Rescue (Propp, 1927).

Internationally, similar concerns are raised regarding the Chinese Year of the Rabbit celebrated in 1999 and 2011. During these years the overall number of stories is relatively high, with a commonly raised concern about the welfare of animals after the "hype" is over. Nevertheless, rabbits have become "the latest fad for pet ownership" in Thailand, according to Kwanchai Rungfapaisarn's 2004 report in The Nation.

Because rabbit overpopulation has inadvertently become a serious ecological problem in Australia since 1890 when the First Fleet introduced the European Rabbit to the continent, it is remarkable to encounter ethical concerns expressed in stories published in Australia and its surrounding regions. In his November 14, 2008 article in the Australian The Courier Mail newspaper author Phil Hammonds discussed the controversy of regulated pet rabbit ownership in Queensland. At the risk of heavy fines, residents continue housing "a pampered black velvet rex or an overweight white angora doe" (Hammonds, 2008). According to Primary Industries and Fisheries Minister Tim Mulherin, the status of pet rabbits was considered in depth when developing the regulation in 2003:

> "Rabbits are a class 2 pest capable of extensive environmental destruction, he said.
>
> 'A decision to maintain the ban on rabbits as pets was made after extensive community consultation.... [T]he risks associated with keeping pet rabbits outweighed the benefits they offered'" (Hammonds, 2008, p.74)

In her August 10, 2007 article in PR Week author Kate Hall reports that "[w]ith the UK pet rabbit population nearing 2 million, rabbit ownership is in third place behind dogs and cats in the UK pet-popularity league table. But various studies in recent years have indicated that many pet rabbits are not being fed correctly, resulting in obesity, dental problems and other illnesses" (Hall, 2007). The story focused on a campaign by Blue Zebra PR for pet food manufacturer Burgess Excel to recognize the growing phenomenon of rabbit ownership, educate owners on correct feeding of pet rabbits, and strenthen Burgess Excel's position in the pet food market.

> "Nearly 700 veterinary practices participated in National Rabbit Week and more than 10,000 rabbits were given a 'Healthy Hopper MOT' - around 3,500 of these were first-time patients. At least 250 pet shops participated in the campaign and the Bradford Excel Small Animal Show saw a

30 per cent rise in entries on the previous year,
and attendance up 20 per cent" (Hall, 2007, p.20).

With a total number of 234 stories, the Ethical category
the second largest after the Environmental one that has 258
elements, and 1.44 times larger than the Commodity category.

B) RABBITS AS COMMODITY

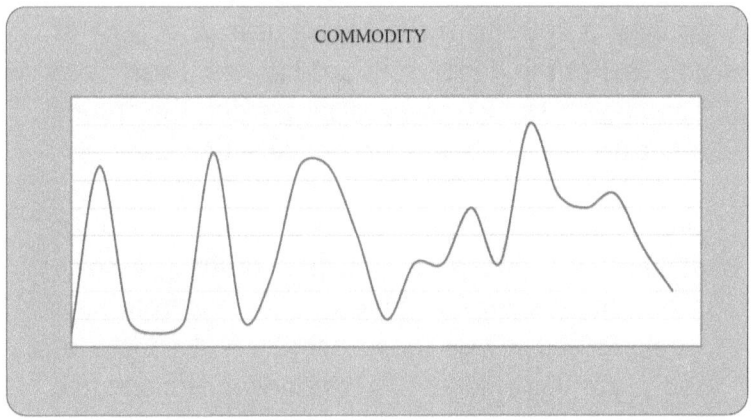

COMMODITY

Fig. 3. The vertical axis indicates the number of stories per year

The most commonly occurring type of stories in this category
is oriented towards food and recipes, persuading the public that
rabbit meat is lean, protein-rich, and economically viable. A
steady peak in numbers was observed between 2006 and 2009,
which can be attributed to the worldwide financial and economic
crisis. Rabbits are frequently depicted as objects of cottage
industry, with some cases starting with adoption as pets and
later resorting to commercial exploitation due to their fast
multiplication.

The narratives of most stories in this category view rabbits
as objects that multiply, thus limiting their roles and functions
to Donor or Prize (Propp, 1927). Victimhood is not seen as such
because there is no struggle or injustice described in any of these
plots; as per Arluke and Sanders, these narratives lack violation
of boundaries.

For example, in a January 11, 2011 story titled *Year of the Rabbit Stew* from the Singaporean daily newspaper The Straits Times, author Huang Lijie begins by introducing rabbits as domestic companions: "They are cute, they are furry and they make great pets." However, the story lede includes the main idea of more and more people "looking to get their hands on a rabbit for a different reason – they love the taste."

> "Rabbit meat imports have doubled, from 1.5 tonnes in 2009 to three tonnes last year. And as the Year of the Rabbit rolls around, restaurants are hopping on the bandwagon by serving the trendy meat prized for its tender, delicate flavour.
>
> One of them is Chinese restaurant Szechuan Court at Fairmont Singapore, which is offering a spicy rabbit meat stew for Chinese New Year from next week. Priced at $198 for six people, it also includes top-grade ingredients such as smoked abalone and fish maw.
>
> The restaurant's head chef, Mr Sebastian Goh, said: 'This being the Year of the Rabbit, I thought it would be a good opportunity to introduce rabbit meat to diners because it is seldom featured in Chinese cuisine here.'
>
> Mr Goh acknowledged that 'few people here view rabbit as food', so he offers guests the option of substituting the rabbit with chicken" (Lijie, 2011).

In the United States, Lenore Skenazy of the Advertising Age praises the entrepreneurial talent of Herman Pelphrey who started a rabbit meat production company in 1911. In her March 13, 1986 article Skenazy tells the story of Pelphrey's personified pregnant pet rabbit Betty-Ann, whose progeny became a burgeoning bunny business where "the brain, the fur, the meat, the feet -- everything, in fact, but the rabbit's button nose" are sold for profit:

> "Rabbit brain powder -- exactly what it sounds like, freeze-dried and Turkish ground -- is the active component in thromboplastin, which is used in testing the clotting time of blood" (Skenazy, 1986, p.7).

Rabbit meat has, in fact, become a by-product of this behemoth who made $10 million in sales in 1987 from its biomedical division only. Rabbit pelts, "which Herman Pelphrey used to bury in his backyard because no one wanted them, now furnish the fashion industry, mostly overseas, with inexpensive fur" (Skenazy, 1986, p.7)

> "And 'if you ever see one of those lucky rabbit feet on a keychain,' says Justis, '99 times out of a hundred it comes from here.' Paul Dubbell estimates his Pel Industries' rabbit foot sales at about $500,000 last year.
>
> But the rabbit meat itself is not about to be eclipsed. Distributing to heavyweights like Kroger, A&P and Supermarket General, Pel-Freez sold more than 1.5 million lbs. of rabbit last year, totaling about $2.75 million in sales, Justis says.
>
> He considers this meat the perfect choice for the '80s. 'With the trend to light meats,' he says, 'rabbit makes sense.'
>
> Indeed, rabbit has less fat, less sodium and fewer calories per pound than chicken -- and more protein" (Skenazy, 1986, p.7).

This story is classified as Commodity because the ethical

considerations regarding the exploitation and slaughter of a domestic companion's offspring are virtually nonexistent. However, it is worth noting that had the story more emphasis on the "pet" aspect of the rabbit "matriarch," it would have contributed to the negative count within the Change category. Without such emphasis it belongs to the Commodity coding category, which is 2.2 times larger than the Medical category that includes laboratory experiments and pest control virus development.

C) RABBITS USED IN LABORATORY TESTS, OR THE MEDICAL CATEGORY

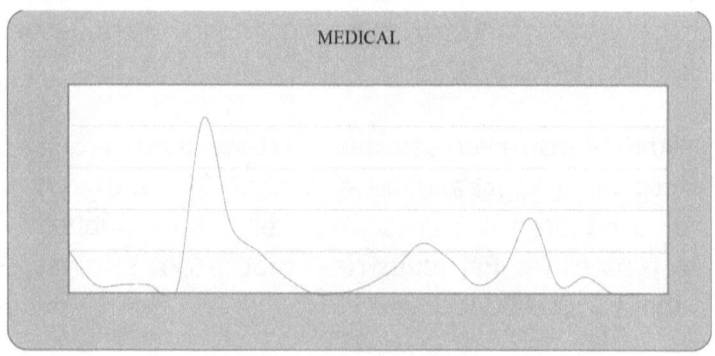

Fig. 4. The vertical axis indicates the number of stories per year

The majority of stories in this category are closely related to the development of biological means against the proliferation of wild rabbit populations in countries like Australia and New Zealand, and the dangers associated with the accidental escape of those viruses into the natural environment.

The roles of rabbits in the plots of most stories in this category are those of Victims (suffering, innocent lab animals) or Villains (destructive pests) (Propp, 1927). Some stories refer to pest control substances "escaping" the lab and threatening non-pests such as domestic companions or wild animals, which allows for duality in the roles assigned to the same species and points at the fluidity of cultural boundaries separating "good" and "bad" animals (Berger and Luckmann, 1966 ; Best, 2007).

After careful consideration, only a few stories focusing on pest control experiments were placed in the Medical category, leaving the remainder of the group in the Environmental or "pest" category where they belong.

The core of this group consists of stories debating the ethical aspects of laboratory tests on rabbits. In the December 6, 2009 issue of Sunday Express, author Ted Jeory discusses the loophole in U.K. laws that allow laboratories to exploit rabbits "trapped in a living hell" (Jeory, 2009, p.35).

> "Animal welfare campaigners are urging an end to licences for labs where rabbits are shackled in 'medieval' stocks for up to eight hours at a time.
>
> They say the Government's 'handsoff' attitude means tests are not supervised properly, leading to suffering for thousands of rabbits.
>
> Campaigners claim issuing high-level licences to labs rather than authorising individual experiments means tests are carried out when not required.
>
> It makes a mockery of the Government's pledge to reduce the number of tests on animals, the British Union for the Abolition of Vivisection said last night.
>
> Home Office minister Meg Hillier admitted the policy after a question in Parliament by Liberal Democrat MPs last month" (Jeory, 2009, p.35).

One of the most disturbing narratives among stories in the present sample is dated April 17, 2011 and published by the British Sunday Mirror. The 502-word report depicts the suffering of laboratory test rabbits in the hands of poorly trained staff. Even the headline sends a terrifying message to the reader:

> "STARVED FOR 30 HOURS, DENIED WATER FOR
> EIGHT... THEN INJECTED WITH DRUGS FOR SIX
> HOURS UNTIL THEIR EYES WEEP; SCANDAL OF THE
> LAB TEST BUNNIES.
>
> Their heads trapped in vices, these terrified rabbits
> are about to be subjected to agonising medical
> tests in a British laboratory" (Owens, 2011, p.19).

Author Nick Owen reports that the number of reported laboratory tests on animals "has soared by 800 per cent from 196 in 2008 to 1,590 in 2009" (Owens, 2011, p.19). Animal rights activists are outraged by these numbers and the cruelty of the tests, saying those can be avoided by using alternatives. Because rabbits are inexpensive and the rules suggesting the use of alternatives whenever possible are not backed up by law, the British Union for the Abolition of Vivisection had to conduct an undercover investigation at Wickham Laboratory, Hants, to unveil and condemn the cruelty of those tests. In many cases the sacrifice of lab animals was not a matter of finding a cure to a life-threatening disease but to test drugs such as the female version of Viagra by pharmaceutical companies like Pfizer.

> "The undercover team filmed more than 100
> rabbits kept in small cages. Terrified, many were
> seen biting the bars of their cages and frantically
> hopping around.
>
> Before each round of tests they were starved for
> up to 30 hours and given no water for eight.
>
> Collars were then put around their necks to stop
> them moving as they were injected with drugs
> through a vein in their ear for up to six hours.

Their temperature was recorded using a thermometer inserted into their rectum, which caused them to kick out in agony. At one point a worker trying to stick a needle in the ear of one rabbit was heard to say: 'I can't, I just can't. I'm quitting - he's already got two b***dy holes in there' (Owens, 2011, p.19)

In an earlier story bordering with the entertainment aspect of rabbits as a real and virtual beings, Kevin Smith of The People magazine reported on Sunday, January 21, 1996 that Hollywood celebrities had boycotted personal care product maker Gillette, a brand of Procter and Gamble, for testing their products on animals including rabbits. The story begins with a depiction of "a fluffy white rabbit with its side shaved and raw from an experiment" that sparked outrage among a "galaxy of celebrities" including ex-Beatle Paul McCartney and his wife Linda, who lead the crusade joined by Oliver Stone, Lily Tomlin, Martin Scorcese, Jason Priestley, Tori Spelling, James Coburn, Mary Louise Parker, Margaux Hemingway and Axl Rose who were "just a few of the 70 big names who last week signed a double-page protest advert in the Hollywood Reporter - known as the stars' "bible" (Smith, 1996, p.12).

"Peta claims to have evidence that Gillette has DRIPPED chemicals into animals' eyes, SMEARED corrosive substances on their skins, FORCED rabbits to drink products and filled their cages with FUMES.

Those that do not die outright are killed afterwards, Peta says, after enduring convulsions, vomiting and bleeding.

In 1993, it is claimed the company used 2,304 animals for tests which included suffocating rats with aerosol sprays and smearing substances in rabbits' eyes.

'For eight years, we demanded Gillette seek alternative testing methods, of which there are many,' said Peta spokeswoman Jenny Woods. 'Then when Woody Harrelson, who is a strict vegetarian, heard about the atrocities, he asked us what he could do to help. He made a 12-minute video showing what Gillette did. It was aired on TV.'

After Paul McCartney saw the tape, he randomly phoned employees at Gillette's Boston headquarters, imploring them to change their test methods" (Smith, 1996, p.12).

The sample used in this study contains 74 stories in the Medical category, which is 3.5 times smaller than the group of stories in which rabbits are viewed as pests or even serious threats to the environment. It peaks around 1995, probably with the raising concerns about rabbit overpopulation in Australia and New Zealand during that time period and the related research for chemicals and viruses to curtail the problem. The Medical category is roughly less than half the size of the Commodity category, which indicates the greater popularity of rabbit products such as meat compared to the use of those animals in lab experiments.

D) RABBITS AS PESTS, OR THE ENVIRONMENTAL CATEGORY

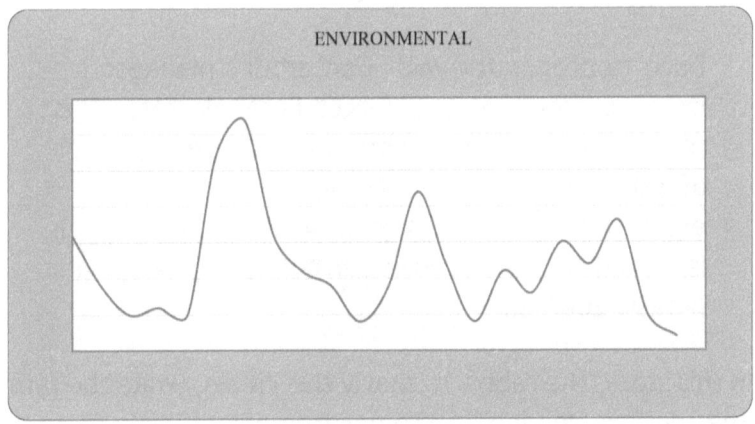

ENVIRONMENTAL

Fig. 5. The vertical axis indicates the number of stories per year

The most frequent type of stories in this category is depicting the menace of rabbit overpopulation and the efforts of farmers and government officials to curtail the problem through the use of chemicals or viruses. The geography of those stories is heavily leaning towards Australia and New Zealand, and the peaks in the number of occurrences are the highest around 1995 and 2002. Only 34 stories came up through a "rabbit pest U.S." keyword search, but the pressing majority of those items are still related to events in Australia and New Zealand.

The most common functions for rabbit characters – normally Villains - in these narrative plots are Violation of Interdiction ("don't go there," "don't do this"), Trickery, Villainy or Lack, Struggle, Liquidation and Punishment. The human characters are endowed with heroic characteristics and typically carry out the functions of Beginning Counter-action, Difficult Task, Struggle, Solution, and Victory (Propp, 1927). One example of a story from this general category comes from The Press in Christchurch, New Zealand, written on March 31, 2007 by John Keast.

"The tyres are kicking up dust in this North Otago paddock. Rabbits have eaten the grass. By night, they move out from the riverbed and do their worst, and here, the worst is bad.

Dave Hunter is the Mid- Canterbury manager for pest- control company Target Pest. He rates this paddock as level four. This means there are heaps of rabbit droppings every 5m or more. At level eight, the vegetation is gone. As it is, this paddock is dotted with dusty holes surrounded by pawprints (Keast, 2007, p. 17).

In this story, the rabbit is clearly the Villain, while the farmers are the victims, relying on the government officials to come to their rescue, using chemical substances as weapons:

"Hunter says there are isolated areas of Canterbury and Otago where rabbits have a high immunity to rabbit calicivirus disease (RCD), still a highly effective tool in controlling rabbits.

But in some areas, RCD is not as effecive as others.

Hunter says there is a theory that some rabbits, from the day RCD was introduced, were immune, possibly through carrying a benign form of the virus.

To compound the problem of growing rabbit numbers, Hunter and Bedford say rabbits, under threat of destruction, redoubled their breeding efforts.

Where, say, a doe gave birth to three rabbits, that number might climb to 10. Rabbits, they say, are nothing if not adaptable.

They say 1080 -- its use is under review -- is still a vital tool in rabbit control, and that numbers will simply explode if it is not available.

From April 1, people using pindone will need a controlled substance licence costing $500, a move criticised by Environment Canterbury's Waitaki councillor, June Slee.

She says she knows people have to be careful with chemicals, but the licence cost will not help reduce rabbit numbers" (Keast, 2007, p. 17).

The Australian Hobart Mercury newspaper ran a story on March 10, 1995, by the Australian Associated Press, which exemplifies the local concerns over rabbit overpopulation in "plague proportions." Even with extensive research, the report claims, "there is no effective biological control for the problem" that cost the wool industry an estimated $115 million a year (Keast, 2007, p. 17). The story refers back to the history of rabbit migration and overpopulation, tracing it back to the irresponsible action of a 19th-century game enthusiast:

Although domestic rabbits arrived in Australia with the First Fleet in 1788, the first feral rabbits were imported from England in 1859 by game enthusiast Thomas Austin.

Some of those rabbits were released or escaped from Austin's property near Geelong in Victoria and their descendants have gradually spread across most of mainland Australia (Keast, 2007, p. 17).

Although the overpopulation of rabbits in Australia was somewhat curtailed after 1995, as exemplified by stories depicting the revival of vegetation in areas where the numbers of those animals had been brought down by various pest control efforts, the problem seems to remain serious even around the first decade of the 21st century with feral "pests sabotaging farms," costing $206 a year, as Nicola Berkovic reports in The Australian newspaper on August 19, 2009.

A disturbing incident of rabbit torture and killing in Vancouver, British Columbia, is vividly described in the October 1, 2008 article by Fram Dinshaw and The Canadian Press:

> "It was a routine night shift for security guard Gwenda Garrett as she patrolled a strip mall on Kelowna's Enterprise Way in the wee hours of Saturday morning.
>
> Then, at around 2:30 a.m., Ms. Garrett saw a truck pull up in front of her, heard the crack of a gunshot, and then saw a man get out of a pest control truck and stomp on a still-writhing rabbit four times.
>
> The rabbit was still twitching, so Ms. Garrett saw the man's colleague step out on the road and stamp on it another two times - yet the animal kept moving - so the man bent down and broke its neck.
>
> Ms. Garrett now followed them in her own vehicle as the pest control truck moved down the road where a second rabbit was spotted stumbling - Ms. Garrett thought the pest controllers had already shot it once - and she heard the gun fired again, yet, as before, the animal wouldn't stop twitching.
>
> 'I just had a bad feeling about what was coming next and I couldn't sit there and watch another rabbit get stomped,' she said.
>
> The two pest controllers Ms. Garrett saw in action last weekend worked for EBB Environmental

Consulting Inc., a private company hired by Kelowna City Council after both local residents and the businesses along Highway 97 called on the government to do something to halt a ballooning population of stray rabbits (Dinshaw, 2008, p. S2).

Although the story is coded to belong to the Environmental category, its main theme remains the concern about a "ballooning population of stray rabbits" and the choice of methods of exterminating feral animals. The mayor of the city had expressed her disagreement with the choice of pest control methods and "said she would prefer to see rabbits being adopted by local residents, relocated into the wilderness, or neutered, rather than being exterminated" (Dinshaw, 2008, p. S2).

Finally, in the United States, a May 10, 1988 gardening article from the Christian Science Monitor published in Boston, Massachusetts by Doc and Katy Abraham refers specifically to the use harmless materials such as buckwheat flour for repelling rabbits and other wild animals:

> "At one time someone told us about buckwheat flour for rabbits. We tried it on our lettuce and bush beans and the rabbits stopped eating them.
>
> But their departure from our property may also have been due to our adoption of a dog that loves to chase rabbits and woodchucks" (Abraham & Abraham, 1988, p.24).

The Environmental category includes 258 items and appears to be the largest one, mainly due to the surge in the coverage of the efforts to contain rabbit overpopulation in Australia and New Zealand in the mid 1990s and 2000s. It is 1.58 times bigger than the Commodity category and 3.48 times bigger than the Medical one. The only category of stories that compares and competes with it is the 234-strog Ethical or "pet" category.

E) RABBITS AS VIRTUAL COMPANIONS, OR THE ENTERTAINMENT CATEGORY

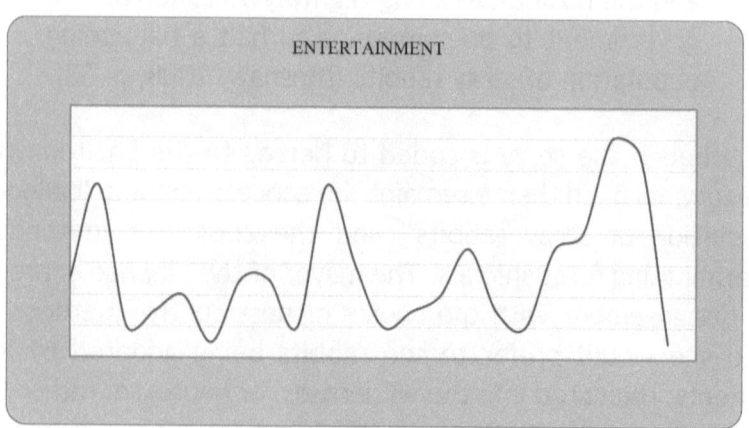

ENTERTAINMENT

Fig. 6. The vertical axis indicates the number of stories per year

The visible peaks in the numbers of stories in this category are in the early and late 1990s and before 2010, but the trends are hardly indicative of any changes occurring in the areas of pet ownership, commoditization or environmental concerns. Since this category is mostly cultural, it would be useful to examine some examples and note the differences between the perceptions of rabbits as narrative characters in different societies. One example that stands out from the rest of the group of stories is a December 8, 2010 article in The New York Times by Jeannette Catsoulis, who reviews a motion picture "Rabbit a La Berlin," telling the story of the animals living in the strip of grass on the eastern side of the Berlin Wall.

> "Part nature study, part cold war allegory, "Rabbit a la Berlin" examines the human consequences of the Berlin Wall through the startled eyes of the wild rabbits that once flourished in the no man's land on its eastern side. For almost 30 years the animals' home -- a 90-mile strip of succulent grass -- was an oasis between Communism and

capitalism, a verdant meadow ringed by barbed-wire fences and antitank barriers" (Catsoulis, 2010, p.5).

Calling it a "cheeky parable," the reviewer considers the motion picture a totalitarian version of the book Watership Down" by the English author Richard Adams: "In keeping with that novel's heroes, the Berlin bunnies -- who bore little resemblance to the plump cottontails of pet-shop windows and children's picture books -- were innocent victims forced, through no fault of their own, to endure the perilous search for a new home" (Catsoulis, 2010, p.5). The plot of this narrative is centered on rabbits as victims, unlike several other cartoons and motion pictures in which rabbits are portrayed as playful, cuddly or even mischievous characters (Albright, 1988).

Outside of the present database of stories, another example of rabbits as victims is the motion picture Pan's Labyrinth, where the animals appear in an obscure role as objects of a hunt by farmers who were first suspected in plotting an anti-fascist rebellion but later proven innocent after revealing their game in a bag. The hunted rabbits end up on the fascist landlord's dinner table, symbolizing his two innocent stepchildren – Ophelia and her infant brother, the human victims of his cruelty (Huppert, 2010).

The database also includes book and motion picture reviews related to a popular piece of English-language literature, *The Velveteen Rabbit* by Margery Williams (Graeber, 2010), in which a toy rabbit comes alive thanks to the affection of a lonely boy:

> "Toward the end of Margery Williams's 1922 children's book, 'The Velveteen Rabbit,' the title character is about to be consigned to a rubbish fire. It's not a pleasant fate for a much-loved stuffed animal, but a doctor has declared him infested with germs from his young owner's bout of scarlet fever. Before the dreaded burning a fairy

> transforms the shabby toy into a real rabbit. Later
> he exchanges a brief look of near recognition with
> the boy who cherished him" (Graeber, 2010, p.21).

Overall, with a few exceptions such as the Isle of Portland, Dorset (Bruxelles, 2005) where a local superstition has made the word "rabbit" taboo as a result of quarry accidents caused by burrowing rabbits, and Australia, where authorities have been trying to replace the Easter Bunny with an Easter Bilby (Foundation For Rabbit Free Australia, 2010) due to the perception of the rabbit as an environmental menace, images and references to those animals appear to be positive in most cultures.

F) THE CHANGE CATEGORY

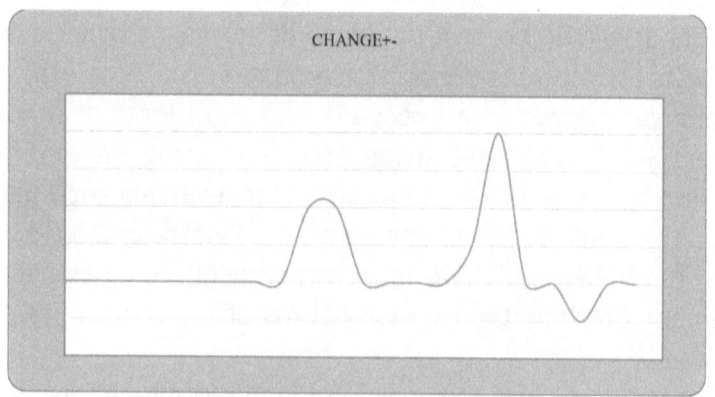

Fig. 7. The vertical axis indicates the number of stories per year

This category is smaller than the other five, but it offers insight into the conditions that can bring up changes in attitudes towards rabbits. The characters and functions associated with the animal in those narratives vary accordingly from Villain to Victim and vice versa. Analyzing the stories in this category allows drawing important conclusions about the ethical, economic and environmental considerations that can potentially bring up change in societal perception of rabbits worldwide. Although elements of change may be found in stories included in other categories, there are a total of ten (slightly more than 1 percent of the total) stories in the database that have been coded as indicating change.

Only two stories in this sample appear to be calling for a "negative change" (Fyall, 2009 and Daily Mail Reporter, 2009) from a Helper (friend) to Villain (environmental threat), but because the stories both refer to the same book, *Time to Eat the Dog: The Real Guide to Sustainable Living* by New Zealand authors Robert and Brenda Vale, "mirroring" the same idea of environmental conservation at the expense of "ditching" or even eating companion animals, they have been counted as a single occurrence. Fyall's article titled *Save the Planet, Ditch Your Pet* was published on October 23, 2009 by The Scotsman newspaper in Edinburgh, while the Daily Mail Reporter authored the story titled *Go Green ... Swap Rover For A Goldfish* in the October 24, 2009 issue of London's Daily Mail.

The authors of the reviewed book express concerns over the carbon "pawprint" of domestic rabbits, among other companion animals, suggesting that only their consumption as food can fully justify the environmental "damage" they cause to the planet. While providing a very specific justification for the cause against domestic companions, the authors of the book seem to have overlooked the massive impacts of factory farming and failed to refer to data about on large-scale meat and dairy production as comparison:

CARBON PAWPRINT
"The environmental toll of your pets
FOOTPRINT (hectares per year)
Alsatian: 0.4
Collie: 0.3
Scottie: 0.2
Outdoor cat: 0.2
Indoor cat: 0.1
Chihuahua: 0.1
Hamster: 0.01
3 free-range hens, kept for eggs: 0.01

3 free-range hens, kept for eggs and meat: 0.007
Canary: 0.007
Goldfish: 0.0003
2 rabbits kept for meat: -0.09" (Fyall, 2009, p.11)

One of the most common motifs in stories of this category is the notion of the pet's image contradicts and challenges intentions to promote or practice their consumption as food (Skenazy, 1986; Black, 2008). That is why these stories are categorized as containing latent ethical concerns, calling for a change in the status of rabbits from food to companion. Those concerned are voiced by secondary characters in stories exemplified by the following 1069-word publication by Jane Black in the July 23rd issue of The Washington Post:

> "Chef Stefano Frigerio braces himself when he puts rabbit on the menu at Mio. It's only a matter of time before someone complains.
>
> One diner scolded Frigerio by e-mail after seeing such a "nice, fuzzy" animal on the menu. Others protested right at the table. It happens enough that the Italian-born chef developed an unofficial rabbit protocol. When a guest complains, the waiter heads straight for the kitchen. Frigerio goes out to make his case: 'I tell them I grew up eating rabbit and that it's my favorite meat. I explain that it's very lean, very flavorful and it tastes great.'" (Black, 2008, p. F01)

Black explains that chefs love rabbit meat and consider it an "elite" meal for its gastronomic and health qualities, but some diners, especially the 2.3 million Americans who keep rabbits as pets, don't. And therein lies a potential for growing controversy. Europeans are more open to the idea of consuming rabbit meat, especially in Italy, where the spiritual truth-seeking, ashram-vegetarian heroine of Elizabeth Gilbert's Eat, Pray, Love (Egan, 2006) proudly orders "the rabbit" among other delicacies chosen to impress her Italian friends with her knowledge of language and cuisine at a local restaurant. Rabbit breeder Bob D. Whitman calls it the Easter Bunny syndrome, which could be one of the factors of resistance or potential attitude change worth exploring in this study. However, one of the most typical transformations from a live toy to steady companion happens in the most tragic of all scenarios, where rabbits purchased as Easter souvenirs are found abandoned on the side of the rode or surrendered to animal shelters (Neill, 2007). Therefore the celebration of those virtual companions or heroes is not the same as treating real animals with ethics and care. The following example illustrates an explicit call for drastic attitude change, and coded as a positive value in the Change category.

In the New Straits Times (Malaysia) daily newspaper, a March 19, 2010 letter signed M.G. D. sums up the basic arguments against the idea of eating animals that are traditionally perceived as domestic companions. Responding to an earlier letter titled 'Eating dogs: Vet's idea, little or no love for animals' (NST, March 17) and to a statement by deputy director-general of the Veterinary Services Department Dr Ahmad Suhaimi Omar that "dogs in the pound could be sold to Malaysians who eat dog meat as a way of reducing the stray dog population," the author argues that "Malaysians, unlike some people elsewhere, are repulsed by the very thought of eating an animal that is regarded as a pet" (M.G.D., 2010, p.19).

> About 20 years ago, the Veterinary Services Department went on a campaign to promote the rearing of rabbits and consumption of rabbit meat because rabbits multiply fast and consumption of rabbit meat is healthy. Rabbits can produce five litters per year of four to six baby rabbits per litter. Rabbit meat is lower in cholesterol, fat and calories than chicken, beef or pork.

The idea did not catch on despite the obvious advantages, as Malaysians felt squeamish about eating a cuddly pet (rabbits can purr like a cat). The campaign to promote rabbit rearing for the table was discontinued because of this. It requires ruthless callousness to set aside the deep betrayal one feels at eating a pet in order to enjoy eating rabbit satay.

It is well that the idea of eating pets is abhorrent to Malaysians. This sensitivity should be encouraged and nurtured, otherwise this ruthless sense of betrayal and treachery could become ingrained in our culture and even creep in to similarly influence our relationships with other human beings." (M.G.D. 2010, p.19)

In a brief (169-word) yet explicit letter, Madam Teeny Teh explains in the January 15, 2011 issue of the Singaporean newspaper The Straits Times why rabbit meat should be banned. Reprimanding the local restaurants that ride on the Year of the Rabbit (Lijie, 2011), the author argues that serving rabbit meat is not only tacky, but also cruel. She argues that that "food" animals are kept in humane conditions and suffer pain, swelling and bleeding, even blindness from living in small metal cages filled with their own excrements. As a volunteer with the House Rabbit Society in Singapore, the writer argues that those intelligent, social animals enjoy human interaction and therefore should be loved and treated as companions rather than being tortured and killed. Teh concludes her letter with an appeal to Singaporeans to boycott rabbit meat, arguing that when the buying stops, the suffering will stop as well (Teh, 2011). The rabbits are the Victims, transformed into Heroes, in this narrative (Propp, 1927). Responding to Teh's letter, reader Wong Chun Han argues that chicken and ducks are also kept in "tiny metal cages," (Han, 2011) but are not perceived with the same degree of sympathy:

"There seems to be some kind of a double standard here, in no small way due to our inherent sympathy for cuter-looking animals like rabbits and dogs, which causes a knee-jerk reaction when their meat are brought to the dinner table" (Han, 2011).

What the author is outlining here is the dual status of rabbits as popular domestic companions in addition to being a commodity, which is rarely the case with most other farm animals, especially poultry.

CHAPTER FIVE: SUMMARY OF NARRATIVE CATEGORIES

The narrative categories described and exemplified above lead to the following logic in classification of the observed news items. At the same time, these qualifications allow for a categorization of emotive and cognitive patterns leading to specific perceptive responses to rabbits as pets, commodity, pest, etc., from audience members.

A) Ethical category. Readers perceive rabbits as pets or subjects of rescue because the animals are depicted as affectionate, docile, looking like cartoon characters or folk heroes, easy to feed, maintain and train. They are also perceived as creatures capable of fear and suffering, thus worthy of rescue and ethical treatment even if they are not kept as domestic companions per se.

B) Commodity category. Audiences perceive rabbits as commodity when it comes to coping with economic hardship in developing countries, and cultures that have traditionally used rabbit meat in food recipes.

Factors such as inexpensive lean and low-cholesterol meat, cheap fur, and even certain body parts that can be used as souvenirs or even medical materials contribute to the perception of this animal as consumer commodity.

The production aspect of commodification includes factors such as fecundity, quiet and docile demeanor, ease of slaughter and the use of fur. Rabbits become an easy source of nutrition or revenue for individuals or cottage industries.

C) Medical category. A number of news items referring to live testing on rabbits in medical and cosmetic laboratories confirm the public perception of that phenomenon either as a negative or an inevitable practice. Reports on the development or failure of pest control viruses contribute to the same story category.

The leading factor for condemnation of laboratory tests on rabbits and other animals appears to be their capacity for fear and suffering.

Factors triggering approval of medical and cosmetic testing include the low cost and disposability of animal subjects and the specific qualities of the rabbit eye, lacking tears, especially relevant in the case of the Draize test.

D) Environmental category. Factors leading to the perception of rabbits as pests include their overpopulation, especially in Australia, fast reproduction and capacity for spreading disease, as well as the ability for small or large-scale environmental and property damage. Cultural traditions of rabbit and hare hunting in countries such as the United States and Great Britain contribute to this perception. It is worth noting that the overpopulation of rabbits in Australia was triggered by their import as targets for hunt.

E) Entertainment category. Rabbits are popular characters in literature, film, and other forms of cultural discourse. Tradition, image, behavior of rabbits as non-violent and docile animals contribute to their perceptions as "cute" and child-friendly creatures.

F) Change category. This group of stories captures: shifting attitudes towards rabbits from object to subject, indicated as a positive value in the story count, and vice versa, indicated as a negative value. Factors contributing to this perception include the significance of tragic events, both depicted and witnessed. Tragic events may serve to catalyze movement of rabbits from one dominant narrative to another, similar to Michael Vick's dog-fighting case (Piquero, et al., 2011).

A recent protest against the employees of a PETCO store in Vestal, NY, who were forced to abandon small "disposable" animals such as hamsters and rats in the face of a flood serves as an example of a perceptive shift from companionship to disposability and back within two days (Fusco, 2011).

CHAPTER SIX: DATA ANALYSIS

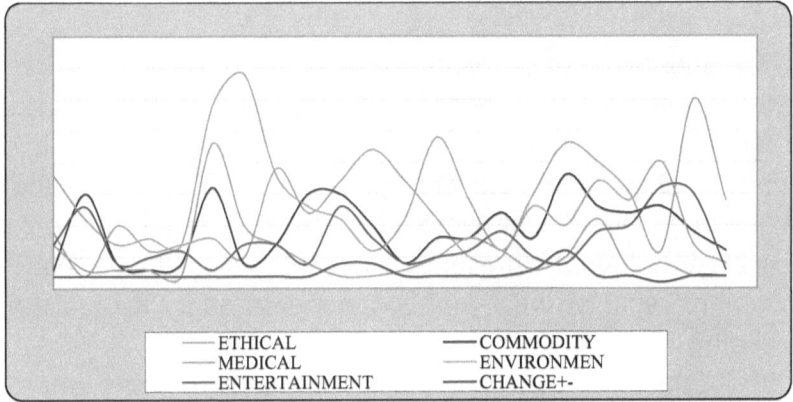

——— ETHICAL	——— COMMODITY
——— MEDICAL	——— ENVIRONMEN
——— ENTERTAINMENT	——— CHANGE+-

Fig. 8. The vertical axis indicates the number of stories per year

A quantitative analysis of elements in each narrative category reveals that the highest peak in numbers of stories per year occurs in the Environmental category around 1995 and 1996 (32). The second highest result represents the number of stories in the Ethical category (28) in 2010. However, the number of stories in the Environmental category proceeds to decline over the years, reaching another maximum of 22 around 2002, while the Ethical category is the only one showing a steady growth over the years.

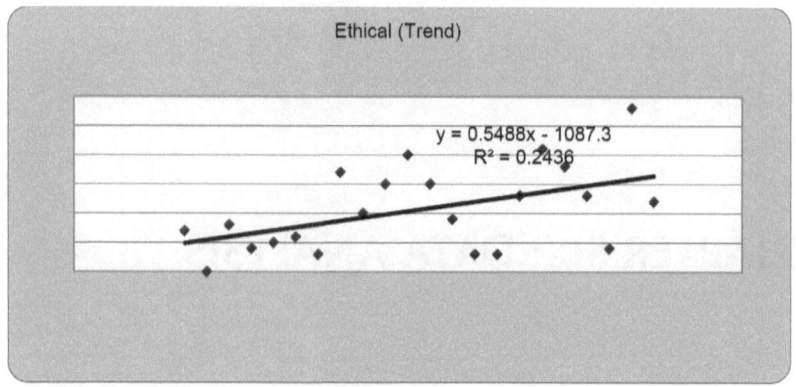

Fig. 9. The vertical axis indicates the number of stories per year

The linear growth of this category is steady with a coefficient of .5488, and no exponential trend. The average change in this category is measured at 52 percent, the median change is -20 percent, with a minimum change rate of -100 percent and a maximum of 600 percent overall. A statistical analysis of the data generated through the present sample leads to conclude that the results are reliable, with confidence measured by R square not exceeding 0.2.

The Ethical category of stories appears to represent the fastest growing group of news items in major world publications, and hence the most popular perception of rabbits as domestic companions rather than commodity or an environmental threat.

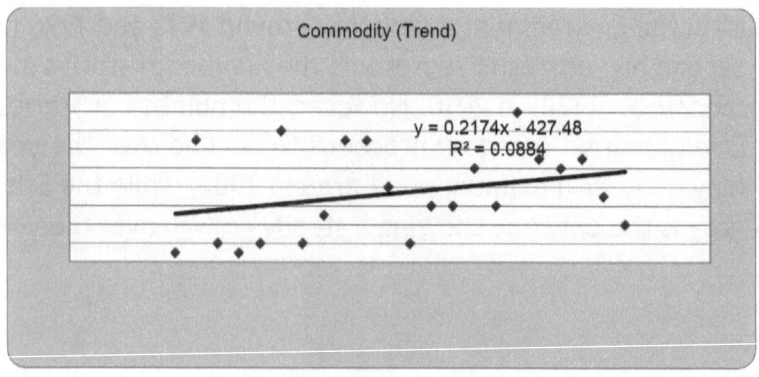

Fig. 10. The vertical axis indicates the number of stories per year

The Commodity category is the only other displaying a tendency to grow with a linear coefficient of 0.217. Moreover, it is the only one displaying a substantial exponential growth rate at $y = 9E\text{-}55e^{0.0631x}$. The Environmental category is displaying a downward slope (Fig. 13) in statistical average that ranges from 3.5 in 1990 to 4.5 in 2011 with an insignificant exponential trend. The Entertainment category has a slow growth tendency with an insignificant exponential curve of the statistical average from approximately 2.8 to 5.

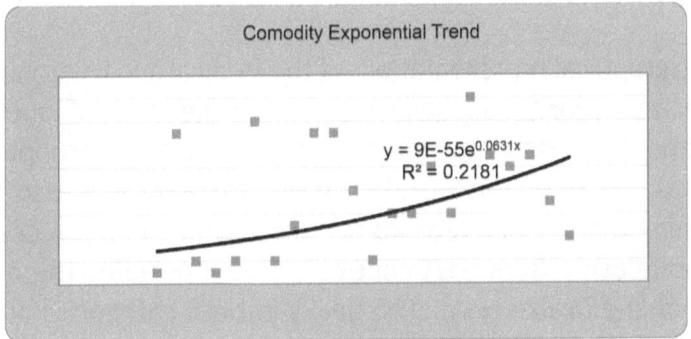

Fig. 11. The vertical axis indicates the number of stories per year

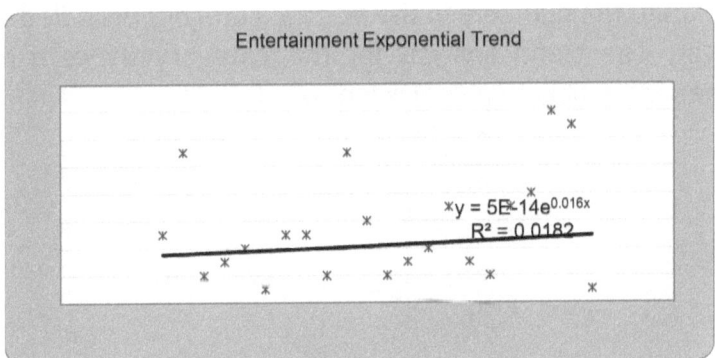

Fig. 12. The vertical axis indicates the number of stories per year

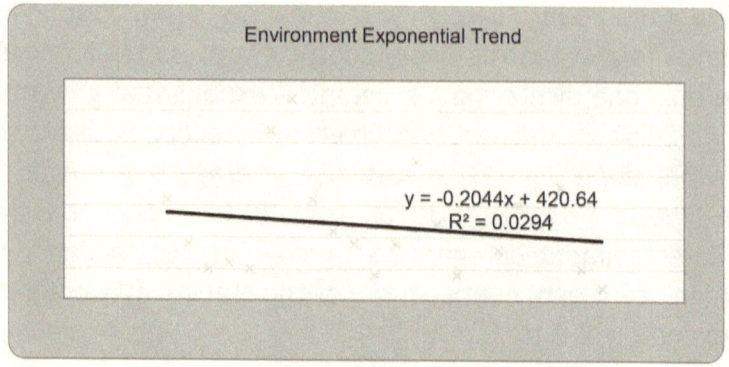

Fig. 13. The vertical axis indicates the number of stories per year

The graphical representations of the Medical and Environmental categories are visibly similar, which can be the result of laboratory experiments to develop means to target rabbit overpopulation in certain parts of the world such as Australia. It is also worth examining the societal reasons for the decline in laboratory tests on rabbits aside from pest control efforts (including the decline in use of the Draize test). The peaks in both categories occur in 1995 when the number of stories in the Medical category reached 25, with 27 Environmental articles during the same year. The next year, however, the Environmental category continued expanding to 32, while the numbers in the Medical category dwindled down to eight. The trend analysis for this category shows a linear decline with a negative coefficient of - 0.1278

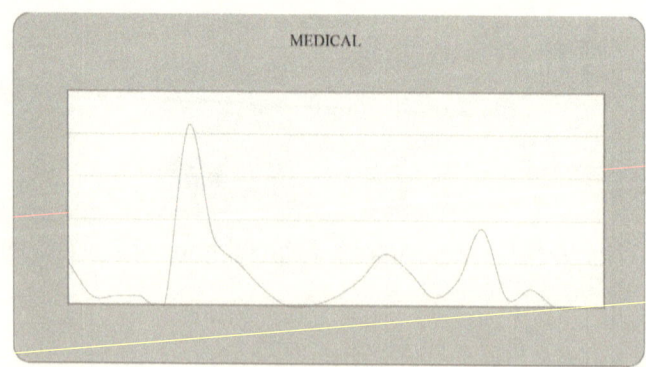

Fig. 14. The vertical axis indicates the number of stories per year

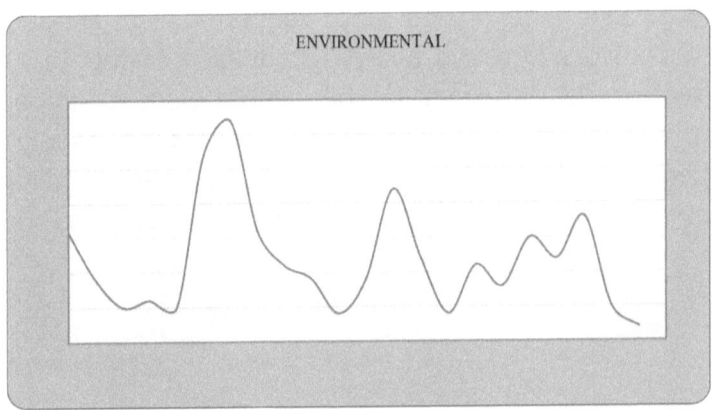

Fig. 15. The vertical axis indicates the number of stories per year

The Entertainment category displays a nearly periodic sequence of peaks and falls in numbers of stories throughout the years, with the highest number reaching 14 in 2009 and relatively close results of story counts in 1991 (11), 1999 (11) and 2010 (13). Noting that this category mostly represents cultural representations of rabbits rather than the status of actual animals, the frequency of occurrence of rabbit-themed stories in 1999 and 2010 can be explained by the fact that those were the Years of the Rabbit on the Chinese calendar. Most stories in and around 1991 refer to rabbit characters in Disney cartoons or Hollywood actors such as Mel Blanc (1908 – 1989) who made Bugs Bunny famous.

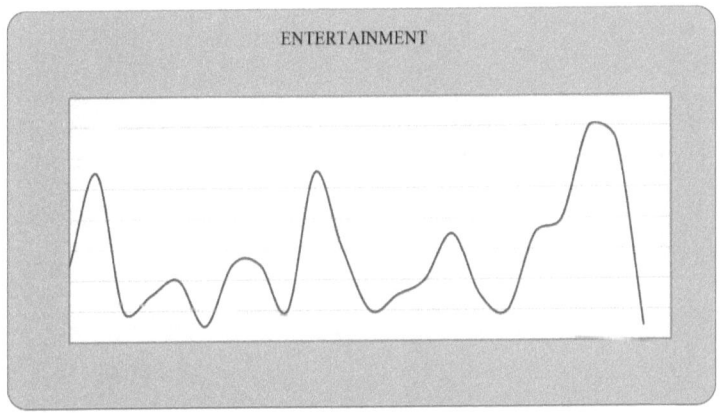

Fig. 16. The vertical axis indicates the number of stories per year

The Change category does not contain enough elements to offer a statistically sound analysis, but each of the 10 stories representing this category in the sample were examined for insight into the reasons and conditions that potentially lead to a perception of rabbits as companions and stigmatizing the utilization of those animals as commodity, or vice versa.

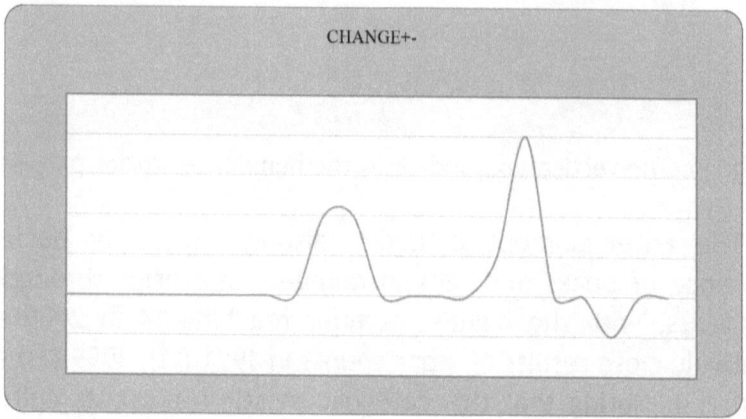

Fig. 17. The vertical axis indicates the number of stories per year

CHAPTER SEVEN: CONCLUSIONS

A content analysis based on the categorization of plotlines of 942 news items from major world publications selected by relevance and arranged chronologically from 1990 through 2011 reveals that the most significantly growing trend in society, as reflected in this media sample, is the perception of rabbits as domestic companions requiring ethical treatment, rescue and care. There seems to be a connection, leading to concerns about the welfare of those domestic rabbits, with the ritualistic fascination with the imagery and celebration of virtual protagonists such as the Easter Bunny or the symbol of the Chinese Year of the Rabbit. The second strongest trend in the perception of rabbits is their exploitation as commodity, which displays an exponential growth rate. Thus the two positions of rabbits in society are in constant competition and conflict, causing confusion and distress among individuals who perceive those animals as increasingly popular companions. In the United States alone, an estimated 2.3 million families have domestic rabbit companions (Black, 2008). In the United Kingdom, the pet rabbit population is approximately 2 million (Hall, 2007). Such societal patterns may suggest a sizable demographic pressure against categories of rabbits as consumable commodities, instead favoring ethical consideration. However, virtual companionship exemplified by images, cartoon or literary characters, does not appear to be a significant obstacle against commodification of rabbits, similar to other domestic or wild animals such as sheep or deer.

The plots of stories regarding laboratory experiments on

animals indicate While PETA and other activist groups and organizations are successfully struggling against laboratory exploitation of rabbits and other animals, there seems to be a need for interference from society at large in banning those practices or at least curtailing them through price regulation or other means.

The present study indicates that overall, the emergence of new moral standards and vocabularies (Lowe, 2006) allows to expect a tendency towards clarification of the position of human society towards certain types of animals, with a steady trend towards more humane practices and understanding on all societal levels. Therefore an ethically progressive move might be the promotion of the role of rabbits as domestic companions and a gradual decline in exploitative practices such as slaughter and laboratory experiments. Community standards regarding retail and consumption of rabbit products, regulation of market prices for live animals, affordability of sterilization for domestic and shelter animals, availability of alternatives such as robots for laboratory testing, and other methods of enhancing the welfare and protection of those animals, while raising public awareness about the moral dilemma of the existing double standard, might help stabilize the status of rabbits as creatures protected by an emerging set of distinct ethical rules.

WORKS CITED

AAP (1995, March 10). Plague proportions: rabbits in the outback Rabbits nation's 'worst pest.' *Hobart Mercury.*

Abraham, D & Abraham, K. (1988, May 10). Questions and answers. *Christian Science Monitor (Boston, MA)*, p. 24.

Alexander, J. (2010). *The Performance of Politics: Obama's Victory and the Democratic Struggle for Power.* New York: Oxford University Press.

Arluke, A.& Bogdan, R. (2010). *Beauty and the Beast: Human-Animal Relations as Revealed in Real Photo Postcards, 1905-1935.* Syracuse: Syracuse University Press.

Arluke, A. & Sanders, C. (1996). *Regarding Animals.* Philadelphia: Temple University Press.

Berger, P. & Luckmann, T. (1966) *The Social Construction of Reality: A Treatise in the Sociology of Knowledge.* New York: Anchor.

Berger, A. A. (2000). *Media and Communication Research Methods: An Introduction to Qualitative and Quantitative Approaches.* Thousand Oaks, CA: Sage.

Berkovic, N. (2009, August 19). Feral pests sabotaging farms -- Rabbit problem costs $206m a year. *The Australian*, p.7.

Best, J. (2007). *Social Problems.* New York: W.W. Norton &Company.

Black, J. (2008, July 23). A Dish That Gets Fuzzy Reception. *The Washington Post,* p. F01.

Bruxelles, S. de (2005, October 7). Wallace and Gromit film cursed by a furry animal. *The Times* (London), p.13.

Catsoulis, J. (2010, December 8). Out of Paradise and Into the Pot: A Post-Communism Parable. *The New York Times*, p.5.

Daily Mail Reporter (2009, October 24). Go green.... Swap Rover for a goldfish. *Daily Mail* (London).

Dinshaw, F. (2008, October 1). Guard reports rabbit cruelty to RCMP; Controversial cull program in Kelowna shocks resident who witnessed stompings. *The Globe and Mail* (Canada), p. S2.

Douglas, M. (1966) *Purity and Danger: An Analysis of the Concepts of Purity and Taboo*. London: Routledge.

Egan, J. (2006, February 26). The road to Bali. *The New York Times*, book section.

Fishman, M. (1980). *Manufacturing the News*. Austin, TX: University of Texas Press.

Fusco, J. (2001, September 10). PETCO discovery: Close to 100 animals lost in flood. *Pressconnects.com* on the web at http://www.pressconnects.com/article/20110910/NEWS01/109100392/PETCO-discovery-Close-100-animals-lost-flood retrieved on November 15, 200

Fyall, J. (2009, October 23). Save the planet, ditch your pet. *The Scotsman*, p.11.

Gamson, W. A., Croteau, D., Hoynes, W., & Sasson, T. (1992). *Media Images and The Social Construction of Reality*. Chestnut Hill, MA: Boston College.

Graeber, L. (2010, April 2). Spare Times: For children: 'The Velveteen Rabbit.' *The New York Times*, p.21.

Hall, K. (2007, August 10). Burgess Excel tackles welfare of pet rabbits. *PR Week magazine*, p.20.

Hammonds, P. (2008, November 14). Pot stirred but pet rabbits still fugitives. *The Courier Mail* (Australia), p.74.

Han, W. C. (2011, January 31). A case of double standard? *The Straits Times* (Singapore).

Herzog, H. (2010). *Some We Love, Some We Hate, Some We Eat: Why It's So Hard to Think Straight About Animals*. New York: Harper.

Hessel, S. & Hupert, M. (Eds.)(2010). *Fear Itself: Reasoning the Unreasonable.* Editions Rodopi B.V. Amsterdam - New York, the Netherlands.

Jeory, T. (2009, December 6). The rabbits trapped in a living hell; Labs exploit loophole in law. *Sunday Express,* p.35.

Keast, J. (2007, March 31). Farmers face climbing rabbit numbers; Pest control. *The Press (Christchurch, New Zealand),* p.17.

Lijie, H. (2011, January 11). Year of the rabbit stew: More diners are trying the meat prized for its tender, delicate flavour. *The Straits Times* (Singapore).

Lowe, B. M. (2006). *Emerging Moral Vocabularies: The Creation and Establishment of New Forms of Moral and Ethical Meaning.* Lantham, MD: Lexington Books.

M.G.D. (2010, March 19). An idea that's hardly worth considering. *New Straits Times* (Malaysia), p.19

Neill, L. (2007, April 7). Consider chocolate; bunnies will thank you. *St. Petersburg Times (Florida),* p.1.

Owens, N. (2011, April 17). Starved for 30 hours, denied water for eight ...then injected with drugs for six hours until their eyes weep; Scandal of the lab test bunnies. *Sunday Mirror,* p.19.

Peggs, K. (2013, August 21). The "animal-advocacy agenda": Exploring sociology for non-human animals. *The Sociological Review.* Vol 61, Issue 3, pp. 591 - 606

Piquero, A. R., Piquero, N. L., Gertz, M., Baker, T., Batton, J. and Barnes, J. C. (2011), Race, Punishment, and the Michael Vick Experience. *Social Science Quarterly,* 92: 535-551. doi: 10.1111/j.1540-6237.2011.00781.x

Propp, V. (1927). *Morphology of the Folktale.* Trans., Laurence Scott. 2nd ed. Austin: University of Texas Press, 1968.

RFA. The Beginning of the Easter Bilby. Online at http://www. rabbitfreeaustralia.org.au/easter_bilby_campaign.html. Retrieved on June 30, 29, 2011.

Rudy, K. (2011). *Loving Animals: Toward a New Animal Advocacy.* Minneapolis and London: University of Minnesota Press.

Saussure, F. de ([1916] 1974): *Course in General Linguistics* (trans. Wade Baskin). London: Fontana/Collins

Saussure, F. de ([1916] 1983): *Course in General Linguistics* (trans. Roy Harris). London: Duckworth

Skenazy, L. (1986). Pet image bugs bunny breeder. *Advertising Age*, p.7.

Smith, K. (1996). The horror picture that made Hollywood hit the warpath!; Stars boycott Gillette in fury over lab test rabbits; celebrities launch campaign to stop Gillette testing products on animals. *The People*, pp.12, 13.

Taylor, C. (2003). *Modern Social Imaginaries*. Durham: Duke University Press.

Teh, T. (2011, January 15). Why rabbit meat should be banned. *The Straits Times* (Singapore).

Tuckman, G. (1978). *Making News: A Study in the Construction of Reality*. London, New York: Free Press.

York, R. and Longo, S.B. (2015, September 30). Animals in the world: A materialist approach to sociological animal studies. *Journal of Sociology*, pp. 1-15.